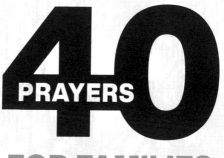

40 PRAYERS

FOR FAMILIES

40 PRAYERS

FOR FAMILIES

Prayers for the
Church or home

DAVID CLOWES

DAVID C COOK

transforming lives together

40 PRAYERS FOR FAMILIES
Published by David C Cook
4050 Lee Vance Drive
Colorado Springs, CO 80918 U.S.A.

Integrity Music Limited, a Division of David C Cook
Brighton, East Sussex BN1 2RE, England

The graphic circle C logo is a registered trademark of David C Cook.

The website addresses recommended throughout this book
are offered as a resource to you. These websites are not
intended in any way to be or imply an endorsement on the
part of David C Cook, nor do we vouch for their content.

ISBN 978-0-8307-8236-9
eISBN 978-0-8307-8244-4

The Team: Ian Matthews, Jack Campbell,
Jo Stockdale, Susan Murdock
Cover Design: Pete Barnsley

Printed in the United Kingdom
First Edition 2021

1 2 3 4 5 6 7 8 9 10

120120

CONTENTS

INTRODUCTION

Having published *500 Prayers for All Occasions* and *500 More Prayers for All Occasions* I was asked to develop a new series of books of prayer for use in small groups or in the home.

There are at least forty prayers in each of these books based around a single theme. Most of the content comes from my first two books of prayer for public worship, but has been revised and re-worked to make it appropriate for use in churches, small groups, the family situation, or for personal quiet time devotions.

My church background was firmly in the camp of extemporary prayer. I started to write my prayers down due to nervousness and on the advice of my preaching mentor who insisted on careful preparation not only of the hymns, readings, and sermon, but also of the prayers. I have long since realised the value of having a resource to be used as a flexible launch pad for my own prayer life which I could use and adapt as I wished.

I hope that is how you will approach these simple aids to prayer. They have been deliberately written in an uncomplicated style and with language that seeks to illuminate the joy of prayer. I have also tried to ensure that they are written in the language we use in our daily conversations. The aim of this is designed to make them easier to 'pray' and not simply to 'read'.

David Clowes
Stockport, April 2020

PRAYERS FOR THE MORNING

IT'S A NEW DAY

It's a new day
all fresh and clean.
It's a new day
untouched and unspoilt.
It's a new day
whether it's wet or fine.
It's a new day
and it was designed by you.
It's a new day
and I want to shout yippee!
It's a new day
to make new friends.
It's a new day
to be loved by you.
It's a new day
and it's your special gift to me.
It's a new day

that I didn't win or deserve.
It's a new day
and I just want to say thank you, Lord. **Amen.**

GOOD MORNING, LORD

Good morning, Lord.
It's good to know you are with me
at the start of the day.
I think because you are God
you must be first in everything!

You made the first day
and you filled it with good things;
all the animals, birds, and insects
were just as you planned.
Every tree and every flower,
every mountain and every valley,
every sea, river, and stream
were first in your mind.

Wherever we go and whatever we do
we are surrounded by lots and lots of people
whom you designed by your love.
You tell us that each of them matters
and you have a purpose for us all.
You planned for us all to know Jesus
and that his love never ends

So I say, good morning, Lord,
and thank you for being with me today. **Amen.**

ISN'T SLEEP WONDERFUL?

Lord,
we simply take it for granted that sleep
    will make us feel better
and though we went to bed feeling really tired
we woke up this morning fresh and ready for action!

We looked out of the window and it felt really good
and a smile of happiness spread over our faces
as we thought of all the things we wanted to do.

The man who wrote Psalm 121 was
    giving us a special song
and he wanted us to know that you
    never go to sleep—
you don't even have a nap or go to sleep in a chair!

I think the man who wrote this
    song wanted us to know
that even when we can't go to sleep,
and we toss and turn and our
    bedclothes are all in a heap,
because you aren't asleep, we can
    know you are with us.

So we want to say thank you for sleep
and that we are grateful that you don't sleep,
which means your love always surrounds us. **Amen.**

WE COME AS YOUR CHILDREN

Father,
we come to be with you as your children
and we come in the name of Jesus.
We come knowing that he has shared our life
and that he has promised to walk with us still.
We come with all those things that spoil our lives
and prevent us from truly living as
members of your family.
We bring all the things that hold us back from
trusting you, our heavenly Father,
as we come to be made whole
in the presence of the one true, living God. **Amen.**

SO MUCH TO DO

You have given each one of us a
really wonderful present
of being alive in your exciting world.
Every day overflows with so many things to try
and lots of new and challenging things to do.

There are new games to play
and new friends to make;

there are places to explore
and stories to read and to enjoy.

There is so much to do with family and friends—
music to which we can listen
and videos to watch;
there are dogs to take for walks
and cats to cuddle;
there are rabbits, hamsters, and guinea pigs
that are lots and lots of fun.

There are computers and video games
    that keep us busy for hours
and books to read that take us to places
    we didn't know existed.
There are emails, texts, and messages to send
and Facebook and WhatsApp to share
    time with our friends.
So thank you, Lord, that we need never be bored;
you have filled the world with so many
    things we can do. **Amen.**

SO MUCH TO LEARN

Heavenly Father,
it always seems that there is so much to learn
and so little time to cram everything in!
There will be the lessons at school—
the ones we like and the ones we just have to do.

We will be learning about things in the past
and more about the world you have created.
Then there are lessons that make us think
and those that are exciting, about
    discoveries being made.
There are activities that keep us fit and strong
and the chance to enjoy fun and laughter
    with friends old and new.
There is so much to learn not only
    about life and the world
but the wonder of your love every
    day of our lives. **Amen.**

YOU WILL SHARE THIS DAY

Sometimes, Lord, when I get up in the morning
I get very excited and wonder what
    the day will bring.
Perhaps I'll spend time with my friends
and play games and have fun.
Perhaps I'll be with my family;
we could go for a walk, watch TV,
    or just be together.
Perhaps we could go shopping for
    clothes or for food.
We might even go to the cinema to see a new film.
Perhaps I'll stay in my room and just read a book.
We might spend time in the garden
    and plant some seeds.

Sometimes, Lord, when I get up in the morning
I get very excited and wonder what
    the day will bring.
But, Lord, I know it will be much
    more exciting and wonderful
when I remember you will be sharing
    this day with me. **Amen.**

PRAYERS TO GIVE PRAISE

YOUR LOVE IS SO STRONG

We praise you that your love is strong,
demanding, and requires a strong response.
When we look to Jesus,
it is then that we know we can start again.
Even when we make a mess of our lives
and what we say and do hurts
    you and other people,
you pick us up and your love changes everything.

Father, we want to sing a song of praise to you
and we long to shout aloud of your wonderful love.
We simply want to say a big 'thank you'
for the way you open our eyes to see
    your fantastic creation
and that you have made it possible for us
to be thrilled by what we can see.
Thank you for your love in Jesus. **Amen.**

FATHER, YOU OVERWHELM US

Father,
we praise you for the way that again and again
you overwhelm us with your love
and that you go on reaching down to lift us up,
to guide our steps, and to help us
      to begin all over again.

We praise you for showing us your love in Jesus;
that your love for us simply knows no limits
as again and again you touch and change our lives.

Sometimes we find it hard to love one another
and we find the cost of caring very difficult.
Too often it isn't easy to forgive
      those who have hurt us,
let us down, and spoilt our lives.
It amazes us that your love for us is so deep and so real
and that there is nothing we can say
      or do that will mean
you ever stop loving us and wanting
      the best for us. **Amen.**

SO VERY BIG

Lord,
I always thought I knew what big
      was—it was obvious,
it was everything bigger than me!

When I was small my parents were bigger than me
but when I got older
I discovered the house was bigger still.
Then I saw a church
and that was even bigger.
The older I got I always seemed to find
something or someone who was bigger still.

Then I was told that some far-distant stars
were billions of light-years away.
I had no idea of how big space was—
I just knew it was the biggest thing of all!

Then when I listened to the Bible stories
and the truth about God's power and love,
it was then I knew for the first time
that God and his love are the biggest things of all—
because God is big enough to hold everything,
including me, in his hands of love. **Amen.**

OVERWHELMED WITH LOVE

Father,
we praise you for the way that again and again
you overwhelm us with your love
and that you go on reaching down to us
to lift us, to guide our steps, and to help
    us to begin all over again.

We praise you for your demonstration
of your love in Jesus,
that your love for us simply knows no limits.
So often we are unable to love one another
and we find the cost of caring too much to bear.
We do not find it easy to forgive those
who have hurt us, let us down, and spoilt our lives.
We do not understand how it is that your love for us
is so deep and so real,
that there is nothing we can do that will mean
you ever stop loving us and wanting the best for us.
We praise you that your love is strong.
May our love for you, Lord, help
us to love one another
and your grace to be sufficient for our family. **Amen.**

WONDERFUL GOD

Wonderful God, we praise you for your
goodness that will never end
and for your glory which grows greater and greater.
We praise you for your majesty which shines out
into the darkness of your world
and for your power which holds everything,
everyone, everywhere in your love.
We praise you for Jesus and that in
him we see something
of your goodness, love, and your presence with us.

We praise you for Jesus' life, death, and resurrection
which means we can know for sure
that he is always with us.
Wonderful God, ever present,
ever real, and ever loving,
we will praise you now and we will
praise you for ever. **Amen.**

LORD, TEACH ME TO LIVE

When I was small, I learnt how to stand.
When I was a little bigger, I learnt how to walk.
When I was even bigger, I learnt how to run.
When I was big enough, I learnt how to jump.
When I was even bigger, I learnt
how to run and jump.
When I was really big, I learnt how
to run, jump, and vault.

Lord, thank you for all the things I
have learnt as I got bigger.
But I have found that the most
important thing I must learn
is what it would mean for me to live
my life for you, Lord.
You made me to live in the way that
will help others to know you,
so help me to learn how to run and
jump for Jesus. **Amen.**

PRAYERS TO SAY THANK YOU

EVERYTHING THAT FILLS MY LIFE

Father, I want to thank you for all
    the things that fill my life
and for the people who make each day so special;
for the fun and the laughter that I
    share with my friends
and for the way I feel safe and loved in
    my home with my family;
for my teachers at school who help me to learn
and for the amazing things I can discover each day;
for programmes I enjoy watching on television
and for books to read that open my
    mind to wonderful things,
for my tablet and Xbox, for Facebook and WhatsApp,
and the way they help me to share with my friends.
Most of all, Lord, thank you not only for making me
but also making me the person I am and
    the person you want me to be.

Thank you for loving me, and help
    me to share your love
with my family and friends and also
    with everyone I meet. **Amen.**

THANK YOU

Lord, we thank you for our parents,
for our brothers and sisters, and the
    members of our wider family.
We thank you for those we have
    known as aunt and uncle,
for that is what they have been to us.
We thank you for those who have made your
    love real and your name known
and through whom you have led us to
    know Jesus as our Saviour.
We thank you for those who have cared for us
and have cared enough to tell us about Jesus Christ
and shown us how we can become
    members of your family.
We ask that we be a channel of
    your love for someone,
that others may know the joy of your love. **Amen.**

I THANK YOU THAT I CAN

Thank you not only for our beautiful world
but thank you that I can enjoy it.

Thank you for the hills and valleys,
    the rivers and streams
but thank you more that I have
    eyes and I can see them.
Thank you for the songs of the birds
    and the music all around me
but thank you too that I have ears
    and I can hear them.
Thank you for the fragrance of flowers
    and the aroma of cooking
but thank you more that I have a
    nose that can smell them.
Thank you for my family and friends
    who make my life so special
but thank you more that I have a heart
    and I can love them in return.
Thank you for our beautiful, fragile, blue
    planet that we are slowly destroying
but thank you more that you have given me a choice
    that I can do what I can to protect it. **Amen.**

OUR FAMILY

Father,
thank you for our family
and for the way we care for one another.
Help us never to take one another for granted
but show each member of our family
    the respect that they deserve.

When any of us are hurting or deeply sad
help us always to be understanding
    and ready to comfort.
When one of us does something
    good, however small,
help us to show gratitude and offer praise.
When one of the family is successful
help us to rejoice and share in their joy.
When our family feels threatened
help us to stand together.
When our family experiences a time of weakness
help us to find our strength in Christ.
When as a family we are afraid and
    face an uncertain future
help us to show courage, faithfulness, and love.

Father,
thank you for our family.
As we remain part of your family
our family will be strong and united in love. **Amen.**

OUR COMPLETENESS

Lord,
we thank you not only for making us
but also for making us in your own image.
We thank you that you so designed our lives
that we should reflect your love, care, and compassion
in our life together as a family.

We thank you for the sense of completeness
that you bring to the life of our family
and that without you there is no life that is real.
You are the source of all that is good and
    true in the life of our family.
We thank you for the strength you
    give when times are hard
and for the encouragement when we are
    facing times of distress and despair.
We thank you for those who support us
    through good times and bad
and for those who remain faithful to one
    another no matter the cost.
We thank you for sharing our
    sadness and our sorrow
and for understanding us when we are
    at the point of breaking.
We thank you for our family and for
    the love we have received.
We thank you most of all for Jesus and
    that through our faith in him
you have freely given us our place
    in the family of God.
Lord, we thank you that in you
    we belong to a family
that knows no barriers and rejects all divisions.
We ask that you will fill us with the joy
and the sense of anticipation of being
    members of your family

with whom we will worship you for all eternity.
In the name of Christ. **Amen.**

THINGS I CAN REMEMBER

Father, you have given me an
    absolutely wonderful gift—
it's called memory!
I think it is one of the most precious
    presents I have ever received
as I can hold somewhere within me lots
    and lots of special things.

Thank you that I can remember great
    times with my family,
when we went on holiday and the sun
    always seemed to shine;
for time with my friends playing games just for fun;
and for special friendships that have
    remained through the years.

Thank you for exciting days learning
    new things at school
and for teachers who were patient
    and had so much to share;
for exams that I passed—sometimes
    to my surprise—
and for the new steps I could take along
    the pathway of discovery.

Thank you for so many, many tiny events and
    meetings that I can still remember
and for people, places, and experiences
    of love that changed me forever.
I can study photographs and watch
    videos from my past
but my memory has feelings and
    I think it has smells.
You see, when I remember I'm suddenly
    transported back to those days
and somehow I experience the joy,
    wonder, and love I felt then.

So thank you, Lord, for the gift of my memory,
for the treasure store of many precious things.
By your grace, help me to continue
    to add to the store
my memories of walking with Jesus, the
    greatest memory of all. **Amen.**

PRAYERS FOR MEALTIMES

THOSE WITH NO FOOD

Lord, from those who have all the food they need,
please accept our thankfulness.
For those who have no food for their children,
please hear our prayer. **Amen.**

WE SAY THANK YOU

Lord, we want to say thank you
for the farmer who grew the wheat
and for those who reaped the harvest;
for those who took it in lorries to the factory
and for those who made it into flour;
for those who baked the bread in huge factories
and for those who put it on the supermarket shelves;

for those who bought the bread and
    made the sandwiches
and for our family as we eat our
    meal together. **Amen.**

IT'S NOT EASY

Lord,
I don't find it easy to say thank you
    for the food on our table
and to know there will always be
    something for us to eat.
It's not easy just to say thank you for
    those who made our meal
or even to remember that we depend
    on you for everything.
It isn't easy because I keep thinking of
    people around the world
who today have nothing to eat and
    nothing for which to be thankful.
It isn't easy because we take for granted
    what, in your grace, you have given
and you are calling us to share our blessing
    with those who have nothing. **Amen.**

YOU ARE INCREDIBLE, LORD

You are incredible, Lord.
You have made our world just right
    to provide our food
and for there to be enough for all—
    as long as we share it!
You are incredible, Lord.
You have given people the skills to grow crops
and just the right conditions in which to grow them.
You are incredible, Lord.
Food from around the world comes
    to our supermarket
and its shelves are filled with all kinds
    of exciting new things to eat.
You are incredible, Lord.
And all we can say is, 'Thank you for
    the food we eat.' **Amen.**

GOD IS GOOD

Nobody asked God to provide our food, he just did!
Isn't he good!
Nobody was worthy to make God
    feed us, he just did!
Isn't he good!
Nobody could do enough to make God
    want to feed us, he just did!
Isn't he good!

Nobody could love enough to make
    God feed us, he just did!
Isn't he good!
Nobody could care enough to make God
    want to feed us, he just did!
Isn't he good!
It's because he's so good, loving, and caring
that he just wants to feed us, he just did!
Isn't he good!
Yes he is. **Amen.**

FOOD, GLORIOUS FOOD

Lord,
I remember Oliver sang, 'Food, glorious food.'
Which I think means he thought
    the food was special.
Our problem is that we take it for granted
that there will be food on our plates.
We don't even think about it—we just sit at the table
expecting the food miracle to take place.
So now, we want to say thank you
    for the food we shall eat
and for those who worked to make sure it was here
Thank you, Lord, for food, our food,
    the food on our plates. **Amen.**

PRAYERS TO SAY SORRY

WE HAVE COME TO SAY SORRY

Prepare a bowl of water and some pebbles.

Father, we have allowed our lives to
be filled with lots of things
that sometimes spoil our friendship
with others and with you.
So each stone we place in the bowl will
be our way of saying sorry.

As each stone is placed in the bowl the person says:

Father, I am sorry for …

And then everyone says:

We are forgiven.

At the end everyone says the Lord's Prayer.

HERE AGAIN

Lord,
you know how easily I make a mess of things
and how often I have had to return
        to you to say sorry.
I'm here again to say sorry for the same
        mistakes I made yesterday.
And I sometimes wonder if one of these
        times you will say enough is enough!

It is then when I look at the cross that I am
        overwhelmed at the cost of forgiveness
and I am truly amazed how freely you offer it to me.
I don't really mean to take your love
        and forgiveness for granted,
it's just in my weakness I mess up
        my life all over again.
I can't tell you how grateful I am that
        you forgive and forget;
it is then that I realise your forgiveness is
        always as if it's the first time. **Amen.**

I'M REALLY SORRY

Father,
I'm really sorry for the way I let you down.
I expect you already know the mess I make of things
and how my selfishness spoils things for everyone.

I don't mean to be so difficult and hard to live with.
It's just I get all mixed up inside and
    I find it hard to change.

So, Father, I'm really sorry that I let you down
by letting myself down and hurting those I love.
I'm asking you to go on loving me
    and helping me deep down.
I do want to be the caring person you
    planned me to be. **Amen.**

FATHER, FORGIVE

Father, forgive us the way we treat the
    other members of our family
and for the way we show them less
    consideration and care
than we often do to those who are strangers.
We confess that we treat our homes
    with a carelessness
that causes others pain and we treat those
    we love with great indifference.
Forgive us our hurtful words and selfish attitudes
towards the other members of our family.
We pray, teach us to see each person
    in our home and family
and every person we meet as someone
    for whom Christ died. **Amen.**

LIFE IS A PUZZLE

Lord, I have a confession to make:
    I get very confused!
I find that my head is full of questions
    I can't find an answer to
which only makes life seem like a puzzle!
I ask myself, just who am I?
What does my life mean?
How will I cope with the scary things
    that trouble me each day?
What can I do so I can keep saying no
    to the things others are doing?
Does it really matter if I just do my own thing?
Then there are the really big questions
that are the greatest puzzle of all.
Is there a God and do you care about me?
Do I matter? Am I important in your
    great scheme of things?
Are you some distant being who just records the
    mess I am making each day of my life?

Lord, I get very confused
and life seems like a puzzle I just cannot solve.

It is then I hear you whisper in my ear:
'I love you.
I always have
and I always will!

I do have a plan and a purpose for your life
and I love you so much I will walk
    with you each day.'

Lord, I realise now I have been trying to
    solve life's puzzles on my own
and I forgot that you are the clue
    that makes my life real
and in Jesus I have someone who tells me
that he is the way, the truth, and the life. **Amen.**

PRAYERS FOR OTHERS

PEOPLE I DON'T KNOW

Lord, I want to talk to you about
people I don't know.
There is the old man who lives down our road.
I think he lives alone because he always looks sad.

silence

Lord, I want to talk to you about
people I don't know.
There is the woman who works at
the supermarket checkout.
She doesn't seem to like her job
and never looks happy.

silence

Lord, I want to talk to you about
    people I don't know.
There is the little girl on the television;
    she looked really hungry.
She didn't seem to have her mum and dad
    with her; she looked sort of empty.

silence

Lord, I want to talk to you about
    people I don't know.
There is the elderly lady who used
    to come to church.
I think she must be lonely as she can't
    get out of her house anymore.

silence

Lord, I want to talk to you about
    people I don't know.
There is that young man I saw
    sitting on the pavement.
He was dirty and cold and didn't seem
    to have a home to go to.

silence

Lord, I want to talk to you about
    people I don't know

because I know that you know their
  names and you love them.
I think you are wanting me to love them
  and help them too. **Amen.**

LORD, HELP ME TO BE

Lord,
help me to be your voice to those seeking answers;
help me to be your comfort to those who are alone;
help me to be your eyes to see those
  who have been forgotten;
help me to be your feet to those who
  are longing to be visited;
help me to be your hands to those who
  simply want to be hugged;
help me to be your ears to those who need
  to know they have been heard;
help me to be your compassion to those
  who feel empty and worthless;
help me to be your song to those
  who are seeking hope;
help me to be your laughter to those who
  need to learn to smile again;
help me to be your presence to those to
  whom you are sending me.
Lord, come live in me and help me to be
  the me you always meant me to be,
that I may be as Jesus to everyone I meet. **Amen.**

EVERY FAMILY

Father, we want to talk to you about our homes
and about every member of our family.
We ask that they will be surrounded by walls
    of love, care, and understanding.

silence

Father, we want to talk to you about those we know
as brother or sister, father or mother, aunt or uncle,
and those who do not have that title
    but are what they mean to us.
We pray, help us to show our gratitude to them
    for all they say and do that is good.

silence

Father, we want to talk to you about families.
Not just our own family
but our neighbours across the street and
    families around the world.

silence

Father, we want to talk to you about
    the family of the church
and the family of the human race.
May we seek every opportunity to show
    love and care and concern.

silence

Father, thank you for hearing our prayers.
Show us how we can be part of their
    being answered. **Amen.**

WE LIGHT THIS CANDLE

*Prepare a set of five candles. Light a new
candle as you begin each prayer.*

We light this candle as we remember
those who are afraid and living alone;
those who feel forgotten
and have no one to help and care for them.

silence

In times of darkness
may the light of Jesus bring hope to the world.

We light this candle as we remember
those who have lost their jobs
and those who are wondering
how they will care for their families.

silence

In times of darkness
may the light of Jesus bring hope to the world.

We light this candle as we remember
the thousands of victims of serious
    illnesses around the world
and those families who have lost loved ones,
as they weep for those who have died.

silence

In times of darkness
may the light of Jesus bring hope to the world.

We light this candle as we remember
those who work in our hospitals, GP
    surgeries, and chemists
and for those in laboratories who are
    looking for new medicines.

silence

In times of darkness
may the light of Jesus bring hope to the world.

We light this candle as we remember
our neighbours and our friends who are struggling
and for ourselves when we feel sad and lonely
or when we are hurting inside and
    don't know what to do.

silence

In times of darkness
may the light of Jesus bring hope to the world.

In the name of Jesus, the light of the world. **Amen.**

BAD DAYS

Lord,
I want to talk to you about those who have bad days,
when everything seems to go wrong
and they are really upset and think no one cares,
as they try to cope on their own when
    they really need someone to help.

I want to talk to you about the children in my class
and how some of them are afraid to go to school;
they are scared of being bullied and called names
and they are hurt by the nasty things
others put about them on the internet.

I want to talk to you about the old
    person who lives down our road
who looks so sad all the time and never smiles.
I think they must be very lonely and
    no one ever speaks to them;
they just sit, staring through the window
    watching strangers pass by.

I want to talk to you about the pictures I
    saw on the television yesterday.

The reporter said they were refugees
and it was no longer safe in their own land.
They all looked so hungry, lost, and afraid
    and they have felt forgotten
by people like us who should have tried to care.

Lord,
I want to talk to you about my own bad
    days when you seem far away
and I don't know what to say or to do
    to makes things any better.
I want to talk to you and to ask you
    to do something special
for me and for everyone on the days that are bad.
I want you to come closer than ever before
so that even on bad days we all may feel
    the light of your love. **Amen.**

PRAYING TOGETHER

Father, we have met together to pray for
    each member of our family.
In your presence we name each one in turn.

silence

Father, we have met together to pray
    for our wider family.
We ask your blessing on them.

Father, we have met together to pray
    for the family of your church.
We ask you to touch them with your love.

Father, we have met together to pray
    for the family of our nation.
We ask you to teach us all to care for one another.

Father, we have met together to pray
    for families all over the world.
We ask that the hungry will be fed,
    broken hearts will be healed,
and that those driven from their homes
    will know your love. **Amen.**

PRAYERS FOR THE EVENING

LORD, TOUCH EVEN ME

Lord,
touch my mind, that my thoughts
    may be worthy of you;
touch my mouth, that I may speak of your love;
touch my hands, that I may serve in your name;
touch my heart, that I may love the unlovely;
touch my feet, that I may always follow Christ;
touch my promises, that I may be faithful to you;
touch my hopes, that they might be
    filled with your grace;
touch my fears, that I may be strengthened anew;
touch my plans, that they might be
    focused on your glory;
touch my love, that it might be a true
    reflection of your compassion;
touch my giving, that it might find its
    source in Christ's sacrifice;

touch my life, that all I say or do may bring you joy;
touch what I think and what I say;
touch my family and my friendships;
touch me, touch all of me.
In Jesus' name. **Amen.**

IN CASE I FORGET

Lord,
as I come to the end of this day
and I snuggle down in my warm bed,
help me to remember those with no home
and who, tonight, will be sleeping on a pavement.
Whilst I feel safe and secure in my home,
help me to remember those who have no home.
Though I have had a warm drink and
    something for my supper,
help me to remember those who have
    had nothing to eat all day.
Though I will probably sleep and wake
    refreshed in the morning,
tomorrow when I wake, help me to
    remember those who struggle alone.
Lord, help me to remember, in case I forget. **Amen.**

ALWAYS WITH YOU

Father,
I began the day with you

as I wished you a good morning.
Now at the end of the day
I wish you goodnight.
But the Bible tells me that you never sleep
and that you are always with me.
So as I go to sleep
I feel safe and secure in your love
and in your promise: I am always with you. **Amen.**

I DON'T LIKE THE DARK

Lord, I've got something to tell you
and I hope you won't laugh!
You see, my problem is personal
and it makes me feel silly.

Everyone thinks I'm big and strong
and that I can cope with whatever happens.
But I guess you already know the truth
even though I don't really want to tell you.

Lord, I've got to tell someone
so I thought it might as well be you!
I've never told anyone
but the time has come to be honest about me.

I don't like the dark!
It feels like being all alone,

as if everyone I know
has somehow just gone away.

I don't like the dark!
I get scared deep inside
and I long for someone to turn on a light
then all the darkness will be driven from sight.

I don't like the dark!
The first thing I do when it's time for bed,
I always look underneath it
just to be sure there's nothing scary there.

I don't like the dark!
So my prayer at bedtime is always the same:
I ask that the presence of Jesus will keep me safe
and that he will light up the deepest darkness
    with his wonderful love. **Amen.**

ABOUT THE AUTHOR

David Clowes, born in Ellesmere Port, left school at fifteen following a secondary modern education. In 1965 he committed his life to Christ at Heaton Mersey Methodist and in 1967 he received God's call into the Methodist ministry. He trained at Hartley Victoria College and gained a degree in theology at the University of Manchester.

David served in a number of churches in the northwest of England before retiring in 2010 after thirty-five years in active ministry. His first book, *500 Prayers for All Occasions*, began as a spiritual exercise during a sabbatical. This was followed by *500 More Prayers for All Occasions*. His third book of prayers, *500 Prayers for the Christian Year*, is based on scriptures from the Revised Common Lectionary.

David is married to Angela, and they have two married sons, a foster son, and four grandchildren.